To Bob, Lois, Cap, Rand, Claudia, Gare, Steve, Rich, Dave, Pete, Bob, John, Tom, Nan, Jack, and Jeff . . . ice cream lovers all. And a special thanks to the Baldwin Public Library staff for their help.

I LOVE

ICE CREAM

By Carolyn Vosburg Hall
and the Food Editors of *Farm Journal*

Illustrations by the author

DOUBLEDAY & COMPANY, INC.
Garden City, New York

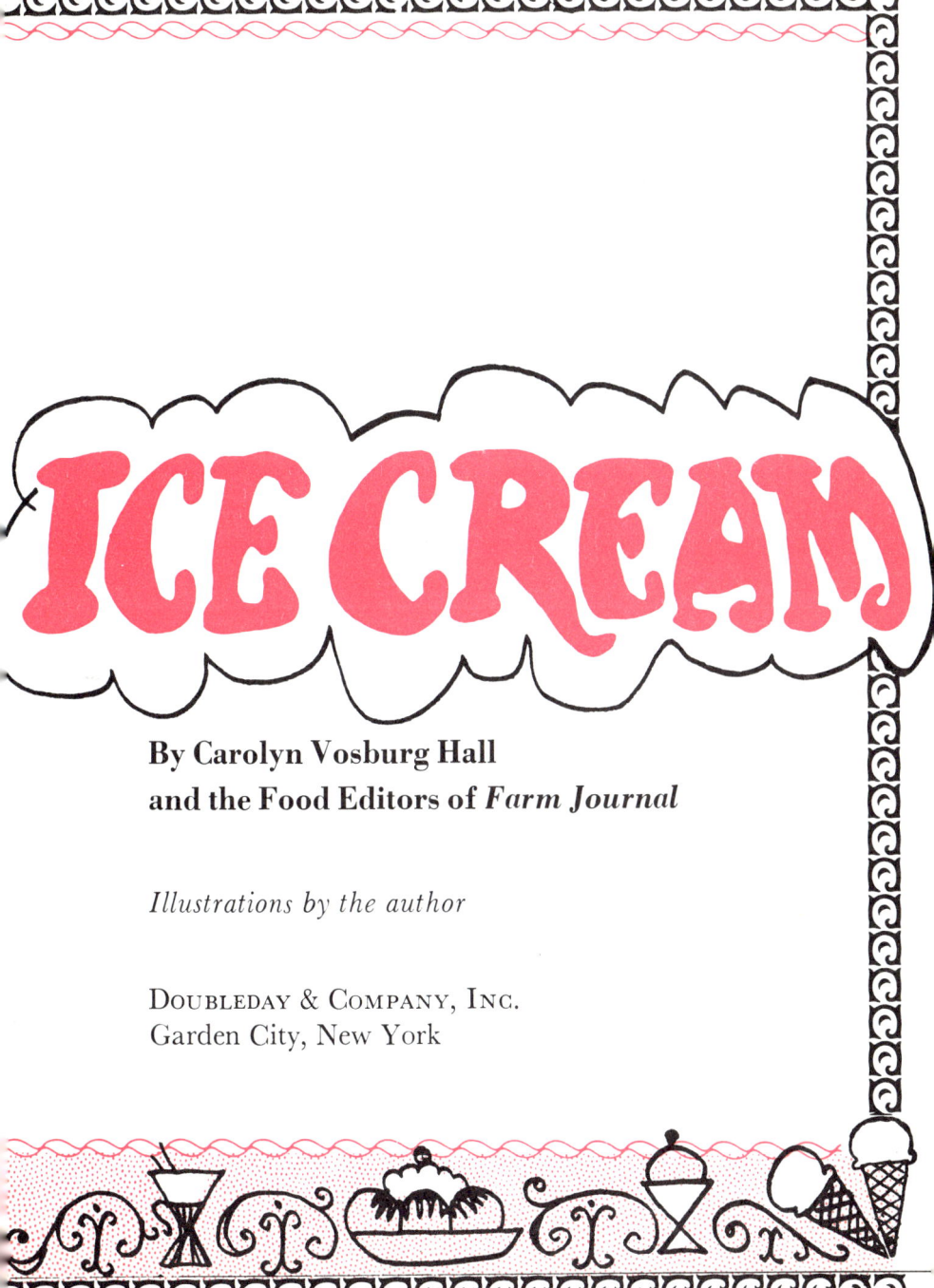

ISBN 0-385-11266-1 Trade
     0-385-11267-X Prebound
Library of Congress Catalog Card Number 76–1040
Copyright © 1976 by Farm Journal, Inc.
All rights reserved
Printed in the United States of America
First Edition

CONTENTS

Easiest, Oldest Ice Cream 8
Let's Make Real Ice Cream 10
How to Freeze Ice Cream 12
What's in Ice Cream? 14
Number One: Vanilla 16
Ice Cream Cookery 18
Ice Cream Inventions 20
As American as Apple Pie 22
George Washington Loved Ice Cream 24
No-Machine Ice Cream and Sherbet 26
Hooray! It's Good for Me! 28
The Ice Cream Machine 30
Ice Cream Has Cousins by the Dozens 32
The Ice Cream Cone Arrives 34
How to Eat Ice Cream 36
Scoops and Dippers 38
Fountains and Floats 40
Belch Water and Moo Juice 42
How to Drink Ice Cream 44
Sundaes for Sundays 46
Banana Split and Rainbow Sundae 48
Ice Cream on a Stick 50
Sandwiches and Snowballs 52
Happy Birthday (Ice Cream Cakes) 54
Pancakes and Pies 56
Make Molds: It's a Bombe! 58
Would You Eat a Moose? 60
Ice Cream All Day Long 62

ABOUT ICE CREAM

Ice cream . . . it melts in your mouth, curls deliciously around your tongue, and then slides happily down inside.

Long the treat of kings, ice cream now can be enjoyed every day by everybody. It has become America's most popular dessert food. *Ice cream is a dairy food* that supplies real food value and good taste in every scoop. Like the fresh whole milk and cream it's made from, ice cream is rich in proteins, vitamins, and the important mineral calcium, for strong bones and teeth. Some ice creams also have nourishing eggs in the mix; they all have sugar or sweeteners for energy, and fruits and flavorings to please those hundreds of taste buds in your mouth.

Long before modern refrigeration made ice cream easy to manufacture, ingenious Americans were shipping great blocks of ice from frozen lakes in the North to cities and plantations in the South. It was packed in sawdust and stored in icehouses where it lasted through summer. When the hand-crank freezer was invented in 1846, lots of American families bought one and learned how to make this "king's dessert."

You can make ice cream the same way today, using a freezer that you crank yourself or one powered by electricity. When you read the directions for freezing ice cream, you will see that it's a big, special-day kind of project. It takes everyone in the family pitching in . . . crushing ice, making the mix, packing the freezer, and cranking it. The exciting reward comes when you open the freezer can for the first taste—licking the dasher.

Most days, you will get ice cream the easier way, from the supermarket or ice cream store. Many stores have gone back to the fine old custom of dipping cones. You can buy ice cream from street vendors, at drive-ins, and in restaurants.

Americans eat more than three billion quarts of ice cream every year. This book tells you how to mix and freeze some of the favorites, including vanilla, chocolate, strawberry, banana, and mint-chip. And it gives directions for all the yum-tummy ways to eat it: sodas, sundaes, shakes, floats, and lots more fun-to-make concoctions using either homemade or store-bought ice cream and sauces.

Ice Cream Fit for Kings

THE easiest, oldest way to make ice cream is to pour cream and sugar or maple syrup —or both—into fresh, clean snow.

In the past, only famous kings and wealthy explorers could enjoy the luxury of ice cream. Two thousand years ago, the Roman Emperor Nero sent some of his slaves to the mountains for snow. They had to travel fast to keep the snow from melting. Nero's cooks poured fruit juices into this snow to make water ices.

Marco Polo found ice cream in the Orient and brought the recipe back to Venice. But everyone still depended on cold weather for ice. Some early ice cream lovers found out how to keep ice in trenches covered with straw.

Creative cooks also learned special ways to make better "cream ice," as it was called. Charles I of England demanded that his cook keep his recipe a secret—to be served only at the royal table. We know his secrets. . . .

Let's make real ice cream!

The goodies in ice cream come fresh from the farm. The cows on dairy farms provide milk and cream. Eggs are laid by chickens on poultry farms. Sugar cane grows on plantations in Hawaii, Puerto Rico, Florida, Louisiana, and Texas. In other states, farmers raise sugar beets. Refiners make white sugar from either crop. Fruits and nuts for ice cream might grow in your own back yard—or in orchards or groves nearby.

EASY VANILLA

4 eggs
1½ cups sugar
¼ teaspoon salt
1½ quarts light cream
1 quart milk
2 teaspoons vanilla

In an electric mixer bowl, beat the eggs until they're light and fluffy. Continue beating while you slowly add the sugar and salt. This mixture will be thick and light lemon color. Stir in the cream, milk, and vanilla. This ice cream mix makes 1 gallon. Turn the page for freezing directions.

HERE'S HOW THE ICE CREAM FREEZER WORKS

Liquid ice cream mix goes into the metal can. Inside is a stirring paddle called a dasher. The can fits into the bucket filled with ice and rock salt. Gears that fasten over the top of the bucket turn the can round and round in the ice while the dasher inside beats air into the ice cream. If your freezer is electric, a motor unit drives the gears. Otherwise, people with strong arms take turns cranking.

Salt for making ice cream, called rock salt, has crystals as big as pebbles. In supermarkets or hardware stores, the bag may be labeled "melting crystals," used to melt snow on roads. You need about 2 pounds (3 cups) rock salt and 20 pounds of crushed ice to freeze 1 gallon of ice cream.

How to Freeze Ice Cream

Be sure that the can, dasher, and lid are spotlessly clean. Chill the can and the ice cream mix.

Put the can and dasher in the empty freezer bucket. Pour the ice cream mix into the can (no more than ⅔ full—ice cream needs room to expand). Place the lid on the can. Fit the motor or crank unit into the lid and fasten it to the bucket.

Fill the tub with crushed ice and rock salt—first a layer of ice, then a thin layer of rock salt. Use 1½ cups rock salt for every 8 to 10 pounds of crushed ice.

Plug in the motor, or start cranking—slowly at first, then fast but steadily as the ice cream begins to freeze. Take turns. It's tiring.

Be sure the drain hole stays open, to drain off melting ice. Add more ice and salt as it's needed.

The electric freezer will have hard going or will stop when the ice cream is ready. Dry your hands and unplug it *immediately* if it stops. If you are cranking, stop when the handle is very hard to turn.

Now it's time to remove the dasher—and taste! Yum. Pour off the brine (the melted salt and ice) and clear away the ice and salt well below the lid. Remove the motor or crank. Wipe the cover free of salt. Take off the lid and take out the dasher. Licking the dasher is one of the rewards of making ice cream.

If you don't eat the ice cream right away, leave it in the bucket packed with fresh ice and salt. Or store it in plastic containers in the freezer.

Ice crystals that freeze from the water in milk make ice cream frosty, melty, and fun to eat. Milk is 87 per cent water. Beating or stirring the ice cream mix while it freezes breaks up the ice crystals. It keeps them small enough so they feel smooth on your tongue. The stirring also beats air into the ice cream, which makes it fluffy and soft.

But it takes more than beating to make ice cream smooth. Milk fat, milk solids, sugar, eggs, and other stabilizers also help keep large ice crystals from forming. *Milk fat* is the word dairymen use to describe the fat content of milk. In its purest form, milk fat is butter.

WHAT'S IN

Heavy cream (whipping cream) is at least 36 per cent milk fat. This is what makes it whip into soft fluffy mounds. Ice cream made with heavy cream has exceptionally rich taste and smooth texture.

Light cream is 18 per cent milk fat. Whole milk has only 3½ per cent milk fat.

Milk solids are what's left after you take out the milk fat and water. They include milk sugar and minerals, which also give ice cream some of its smoothness and body.

Sugar enhances the flavor of ice cream. Too much sugar lowers the freezing point—the ice cream takes longer to freeze.

Eggs bind all the ingredients together and make ice cream smooth.

Stabilizers add smoothness, too. Some home recipes call for gelatin or flour. Chemists for the dairy industry have formulated other stabilizers and emulsifiers for commercial ice cream makers. They help ice cream resist melting, survive temperature changes, and keep longer.

Adding rock salt to the ice helps ice cream freeze faster. It makes a brine that is colder than ice. However, if you use too much rock salt, the ice cream freezes too fast and gets grainy. If you don't use enough rock salt, ice cream takes forever to freeze. Follow the recipe! ❄

ICE CREAM?

How you crank the freezer is important. If you rest for even a few minutes, big ice crystals form. You need helpers to keep it going. If ice cream thaws and refreezes, that makes large ice crystals—so keep it cold.

NUMBER ONE

Vanilla is the all-time favorite ice cream flavor. You can make other flavors from this recipe, too (see page 20).

VANILLA

1½ cups sugar
2 tablespoons flour
½ teaspoon salt
1 quart milk
4 eggs, beaten
1 quart light cream
2 tablespoons vanilla

Stir the sugar, flour, and salt together in a 3-quart heavy saucepan. Stir in about ½ cup milk. Gradually add remaining milk and stir in the beaten eggs. Place pan over medium heat and cook, stirring constantly, until mixture thickens slightly.

Chill the mixture in the refrigerator. Stir the cream and vanilla into the cooled mixture and freeze, following directions on pages 12 and 13.

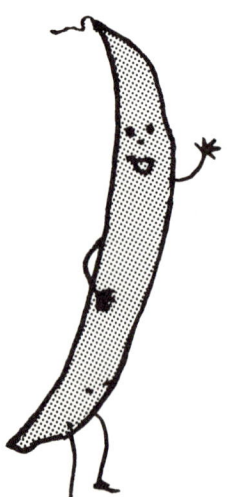

I am a vanilla bean from Mexico. I grow to be 5 to 10 inches tall. Then I'm dried, chopped and perked (like coffee) to make the great flavoring used in lots of cooking.

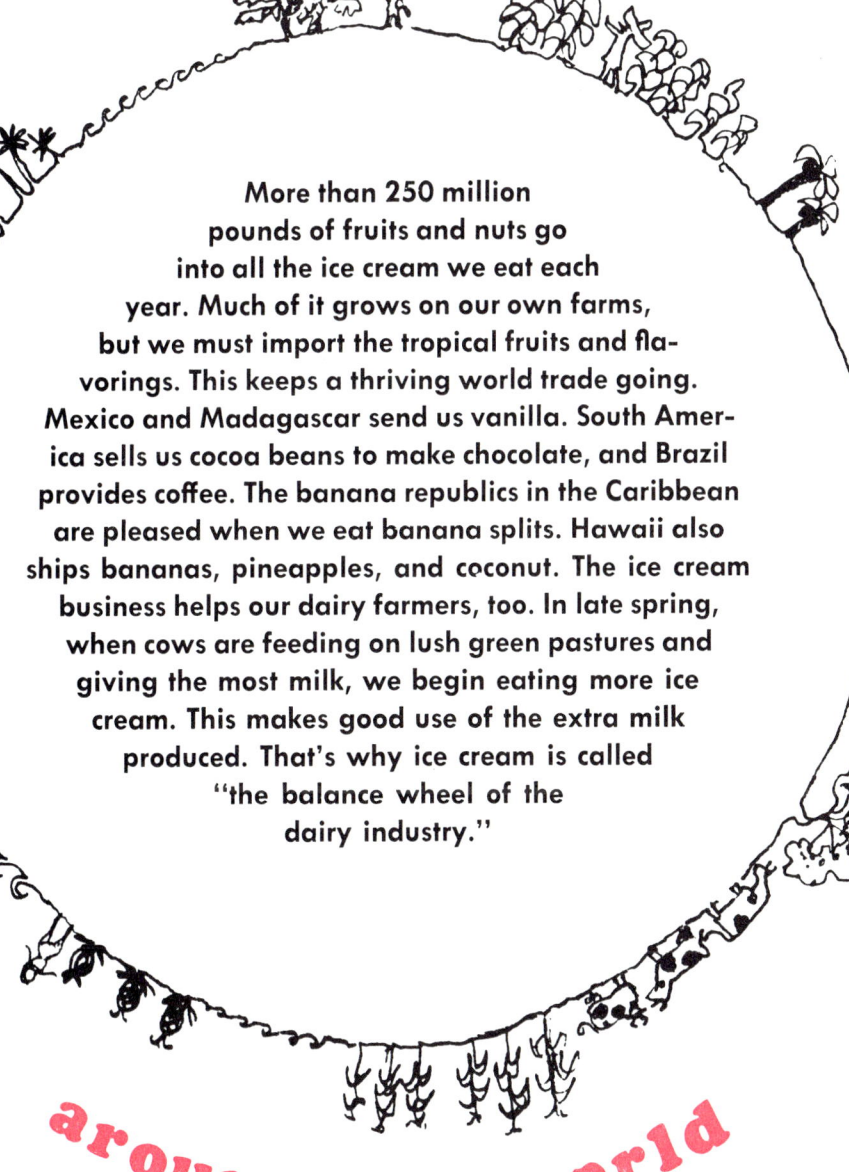

More than 250 million pounds of fruits and nuts go into all the ice cream we eat each year. Much of it grows on our own farms, but we must import the tropical fruits and flavorings. This keeps a thriving world trade going. Mexico and Madagascar send us vanilla. South America sells us cocoa beans to make chocolate, and Brazil provides coffee. The banana republics in the Caribbean are pleased when we eat banana splits. Hawaii also ships bananas, pineapples, and coconut. The ice cream business helps our dairy farmers, too. In late spring, when cows are feeding on lush green pastures and giving the most milk, we begin eating more ice cream. This makes good use of the extra milk produced. That's why ice cream is called "the balance wheel of the dairy industry."

around the world

Ice Cream Cookery

Strange as it seems, some cold foods need cooking first. Many people like best the kind of ice cream made from a cooked custard mixture. A custard must be cooked slowly and carefully in a heavy saucepan so it won't scorch or curdle.

Mix the custard following the recipe on page 16. Put it over medium-low heat and never stop stirring it. Use a wooden spoon so the handle doesn't get hot. Stir the bottom of the pan in a figure eight to keep all the custard in motion so it will cook evenly without getting lumps.

If it cooks too fast and makes lumps or tiny curdles of cooked egg white, quickly take the pan off heat. Have a wire whisk or egg beater handy so you can beat the mixture smooth again.

Ice cream custard is done when it's slightly thickened. Do not let it come to a boil.

Pour cooked custard into a bowl and press a sheet of plastic wrap over the surface to prevent skin from forming. Chill in the refrigerator. The colder it is when you put it in the freezer, the faster it will freeze.

The Kitchen Code

Everyone who handles dairy products must be super-clean. Germs grow rapidly in anything creamy. So scrub and scald the ice cream can, lid, and dasher carefully each time you use it.

Keep your work area clean and neat, too. Spilled sugar is like sand, and wet sugar is like glue. Mop it up. Twice! Get out all the tools, pans, bowls, and supplies you need before you start to cook. Put things away as you finish using them.

APPLIANCES

Plug in electric appliances so that no one can trip over the cords. Dry your hands before you plug anything in or out—water conducts electricity. Turn pan handles in over the stove so that no one bumps them off. Read instruction books before you use ice cream freezers or mixers or blenders and be wary of whirring blades.

But the big thing for ice cream lovers to remember is: CLOSE THE FREEZER DOOR FIRMLY after you get ice cream. Cold air leaks out quickly and thaws everything inside. You'll have ice cream soup, spongy vegetables—and a mad mom!

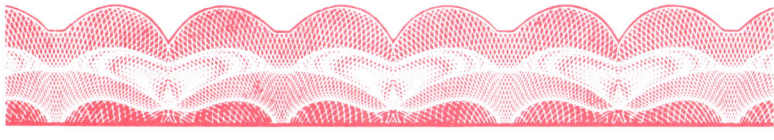

ce cream

Vanilla and chocolate are the two favorite American flavors. Strawberry used to be third, but now more people ask for ripples or combinations. Neapolitan, a popular combination, is called van-choc-straw in some parts of the country.

And there are hundreds of other flavors to titillate your taste buds: banana, maple nut, lemon, peppermint, peach, and mm-many more.

Some flavors are big in some parts of the country. Easterners love coffee ice cream. Butter pecan is popular where pecans grow. One famous chain of ice cream stores brags of their experiments with 431 flavors!

To taste good, a recipe has to have the right amounts of liquids, fruits, and sweeteners. If you add sweet stuff like peanut brittle, for example, you have to cut down on sugar in the basic recipe. The recipes here tell how to change Good Old Number 1 Vanilla on page 16 into other flavors.

CHOCOLATE: Mix ⅔ cup cocoa (unsweetened) with the sugar in the saucepan before adding liquid.

nventions

CHOCOLATE MINT-CHIP: Omit the vanilla. Add 1 teaspoon peppermint extract, 1 cup mini-size chocolate chips, and ½ teaspoon green food coloring before freezing.

STRAWBERRY: Use only 3 cups milk and 3 cups light cream. Thaw and mash 2 (10-ounce) packages frozen strawberries; add before freezing.

BANANA: Use only 3 cups milk and 3 cups light cream. Add 2 cups mashed banana (4 to 5 ripe bananas) before freezing.

BUTTER PECAN: Sauté 1½ cups broken pecan pieces in ¼ cup butter. Sprinkle with ½ teaspoon salt. Add to mix before freezing.

PEPPERMINT STICK: Decrease the sugar to 1 cup. Add ½ cup crushed peppermint candy to ingredients in saucepan. Add another ½ cup crushed peppermint to the cooled mixture before freezing.

PEANUT BRITTLE: Decrease the sugar to 1 cup. Add 1 cup crushed peanut brittle before freezing.

Americans love ice cream. We eat more of it than anyone else in the world. If you average out the big ice cream eaters with the non-ice cream eaters, each one of us eats 30 pints a year.

Ice cream has the amazing ability to change flavors. Famous ice cream companies keep inventing tempting new flavors. Agricultural college professors and students also experiment with home-grown fruits and foods. They've even made a good pumpkin pie ice cream! If you ever visit a campus with a dairy school, ask if they have a store—and go get a cone.

Ice cream is a real food and a delightful way to get the milk you need. It's a perfect snack, and it fancies up the plainest meal. This fun food cheers sick people, and busy people can eat it on the run. The government makes ice cream for our military men and women all over the world.

"As American as Ice Cream and Apple Pie"

The cold soft texture of ice cream goes well with other foods. It's especially good with America's other old-time favorite, apple pie. Pie à la mode is partly a French phrase that means with ice cream, or "in the fashion."

George Washington Loved Ice Cream

You don't need a machine to make ice cream. Make it the way they did in George Washington's time. His cooks used two pewter bowls to freeze ice cream. The smaller bowl, filled with ice cream mix, nestled in the larger bowl, packed with ice and salt. One cook stirred the ice cream while the other shook the bowl in the ice.

GEORGE WASHINGTON'S ICE CREAM

It may seem like all day, but it only takes about 20 minutes to freeze a small juice can of ice cream, stirring the way they did then.

- ⅓ cup sugar
- A few grains of salt
- 1⅔ cups whole milk
- 1 egg, beaten
- ¾ teaspoon vanilla

Mix together the sugar, salt, milk, and egg in a small saucepan. Cook on medium heat, stirring all the time, until the mix reaches 180° on a candy thermometer. Take it off heat and add the vanilla. Chill the mix overnight so it's really cold when you begin to freeze it. Makes 5 juice cans full.

For your own mini-ice cream freezer, use a 6-ounce metal juice can for the ice cream mix and a bigger container for the ice—a half-gallon milk carton with the top cut off. Fill the carton with 2 parts of crushed ice to 1 part rock salt. Fill the juice can ⅔ full of mix and push it into the ice. Stir with a fork until it freezes.

Dolley Madison was the first President's wife to serve ice cream in the White House. She delighted and impressed guests at state functions with her "large shiny dome of pink ice cream." But it took many White House servants, shaking and stirring most of the day, to freeze it.

About fifty years later, in 1846, a woman named Nancy Johnson invented the hand-crank freezer. This machine simplified ice cream making, but to have ice in the summer, men had to harvest it in the winter and bury it in straw in icehouses—or wait for a summer hailstorm. In the 1920s mechanical refrigerators and freezers were perfected. Now you can make ice in your home freezer.

No Machine Ice Cream

Make ice cream in your freezer or refrigerator. This recipe makes 2 trays full.

- 6 eggs
- 1 cup sugar
- 2 cups milk
- 2 teaspoons vanilla
- ½ teaspoon salt
- 2 cups heavy cream

Beat the eggs with an egg beater or electric mixer until thick and lemon-colored. Add the sugar, milk, vanilla, and salt. Blend well. Whip the cream in a large chilled bowl. Fold in the egg mixture. Pour into 2 cold refrigerator trays. Freeze until it's set enough to break into chunks. Put the chunks in a large chilled bowl. Beat with egg beater or mixer until light and fluffy but not melted. Pour back into trays and freeze until firm.

Let it "mellow" in the refrigerator section before you serve it, about 30 minutes. Each tray makes 4 servings.

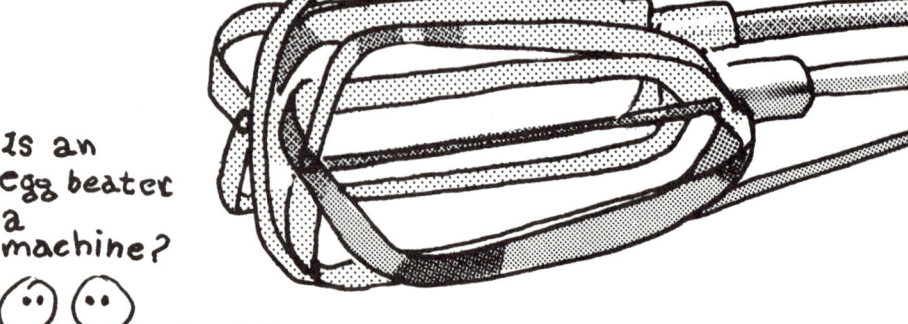

Is an egg beater a machine? I don't know

Favorite Fruit Sherbet

  1 cup mashed strawberries, pineapple, peaches, pears, or other fruit
  1 mashed ripe banana
  Juice of 1 lemon
  Juice of 1 orange
  1 cup sugar
  1 cup light cream

In a large bowl, beat all the ingredients together with an egg beater until thoroughly blended. Pour into a refrigerator tray and freeze 1 hour. Take the tray out of the freezing compartment and stir the sherbet in the tray. Put it back to freeze 1 hour longer, or until firm. Makes 6 servings.

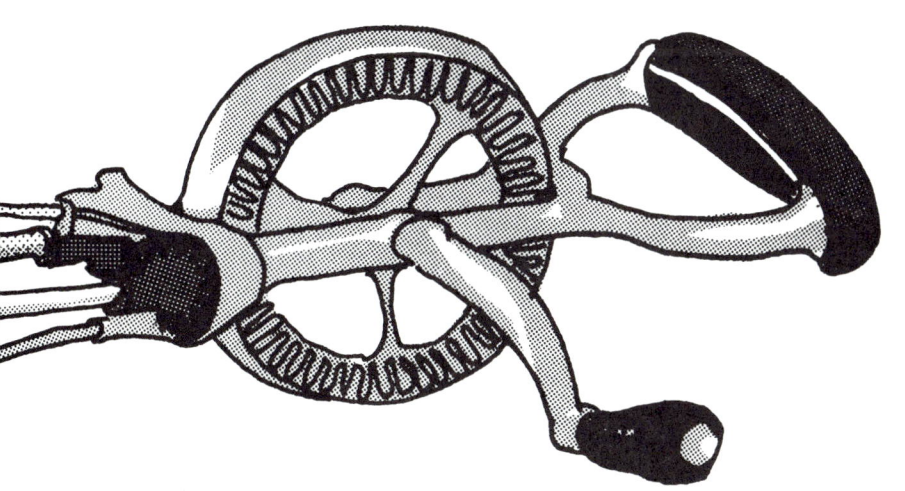

Ice cream supplies all the same good food values as the milk, cream, eggs, and sugar that go into it. None of the proteins, minerals, or vitamins get lost when you mix these foods together and make ice cream.

The milk solids in ice cream include calcium. Lifelong, our bodies need a good supply of this essential mineral, necessary for strong bones and teeth. We also need calcium to clot blood and make nerves and muscles work. If we don't get enough calcium every day, our bodies steal it from our bones and they get brittle.

A surprising fact is that no single nutrient can function properly all by itself. For example, calcium can't be used in the body without some help from vitamin D. Milk today is enriched with this important vitamin. Milk and ice cream both give you the calcium you need to keep your bones happy. Milk is also a good source of B vitamins riboflavin and thiamin, which give you pep and help you use food to grow.

The milk and eggs in ice cream provide protein to build muscles, make red blood, and fight off germs. Cream carries a rich supply of vitamin A to make soft smooth skin and bright eyes.

Cream is a fat that our bodies burn as a fuel for energy. Sugar and fruits are also energy foods, called carbohydrates. The energy value of fats and carbohydrates is measured in calories. Ice cream gives you a healthy lot of calories. Depending on the amount of milk fat in it, 1 cup of ice cream has from 255 to 330 calories. A cup of ice milk has 200 calories and a cup of sherbet, 260 calories.

THE ICE CREAM

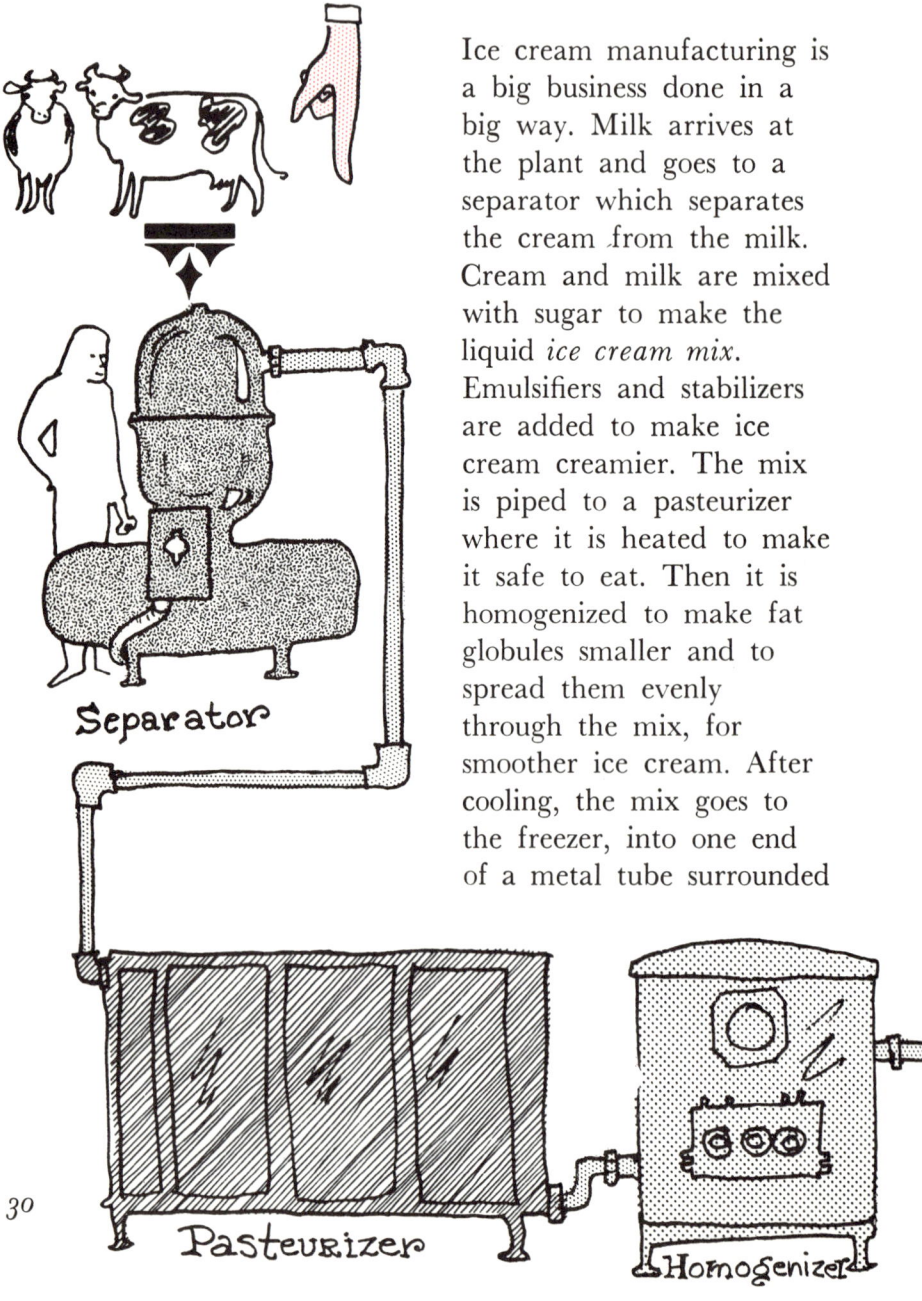

Ice cream manufacturing is a big business done in a big way. Milk arrives at the plant and goes to a separator which separates the cream from the milk. Cream and milk are mixed with sugar to make the liquid *ice cream mix*. Emulsifiers and stabilizers are added to make ice cream creamier. The mix is piped to a pasteurizer where it is heated to make it safe to eat. Then it is homogenized to make fat globules smaller and to spread them evenly through the mix, for smoother ice cream. After cooling, the mix goes to the freezer, into one end of a metal tube surrounded

MACHINE

by coolant. The mix shoots through the tube under pressure and comes out semifrozen. Rotating blades inside the tube whip air into the mix. Manufacturers call the air "overrun," and they can regulate how much air they whip in. Without air, ice cream would be a solid lump. Too much air is forbidden by law. Who wants to buy a box full of air? Nuts and fruits are added to soft-frozen ice cream before it's packaged. The packages are stored in the hardening room—a big freezer kept at 20 degrees below zero. Refrigerated trucks take it to stores.

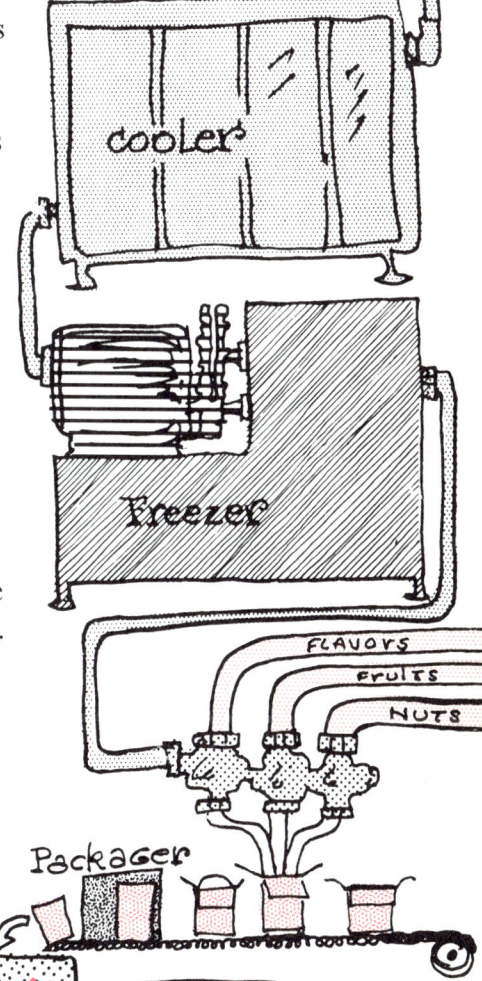

ICE CREAM HAS COUSINS BY THE DOZENS

Not all the stuff in the grocery store freezer is ice cream. Look at all those other frosty desserts. Here's how you know what's what:

ICE CREAM: The government says that ice *cream* must contain at least 10 per cent milk fat and 20 per cent milk solids. A gallon must weigh at least 4½ pounds, a quart 18 ounces.

FRENCH ICE CREAM: When eggs or egg yolk solids are added to the ice cream mix, it is called French or French custard ice cream.

ICE MILK: Frozen and flavored like ice cream, ice milk contains all the high-quality nutrients found in whole milk, including from 2 to 7 per cent milk fat.

FRUIT SHERBET: Fruits and fruit acid are what make sherbet taste so fresh and tart. Compared with ice cream, sherbet has less milk and less air whipped in, and more sugar.

WATER ICE: This is sherbet without milk.

MELLORINE: This frozen dessert contains milk solids, but no milk fat. It substitutes vegetable fats like soybean or cottonseed oil.

Taste is the best way to judge ice cream, since quality and richness vary from brand to brand. The "hand-packed" ice cream—the kind dipped for cones in ice cream stores—is usually richer. It has as much as 14 to 18 per cent milk fat, and less air is beaten into it. Taste. If it's rich, fresh-tasting, and creamy, you'll know.

In packages, the higher-quality ice cream weighs more than minimum standard because it has less air or, as manufacturers say, "low overrun."

The ice cream family comes in all kinds and sizes of packages. . . .

The Ice Cream Cone Arrives

The ice cream cone is the perfect ecology package. You eat it all.

Who thought up such a good idea? Most historians agree that it happened at the St. Louis World's Fair in 1904. The story is that one of the many ice cream stands at the fair ran out of dishes on a very hot day. The waffle seller in the next booth rolled a waffle cone for the ice cream. It was an immediate hit and the two happy men named it "The World's Fair Cornucopia."

Inventors scrambled to design unusual cones. Some had side pouches for two dips, some were spiral, some had flat bottoms to sit on the table, and some had special molded drip channels.

Nowadays, you can choose between a crunchy sugar cone that looks like a thin rolled waffle, or a lighter cone baked in a mold.

The crispy, crunchy cone goes well with the cold softness of ice cream. To be fancy, add a coating of nuts or candy sprinkles. Push the ice cream cone upside down into a bowl of finely chopped nuts or tiny cake decorating candies. Chocolate jimmies or confetti wafers have a party look. Or sprinkle ice cream with fruit-flavor gelatin crystals. Or make a clown face with gumdrops.

Super duper triple scooper

Hey! A clown face cone!

HOW TO

Ice cream cones inspire imaginative ways to eat ice cream. A first, fast lick around the rim catches any drips. Then some slow savoring tonguefuls up the sides, followed by shaping strokes circling the whole dip. A hot day speeds ice cream cone eating into a contest between artistic perfection in licking style, and the need to catch the fast-melting drips on a soggy cone.

Everyone develops his own special style in eating ice cream. Some ice cream lovers say that firm bites give the greatest pleasure, testing teeth against the sudden cold.

When ice cream comes in bowls, technique changes. Here, some prefer dainty lip sips from the spoon tips. Others like to smother a big spoonful in their mouths until it melts. Kids like to play "Ugly Eaters" and squish it back and forth through their teeth. And some enjoy stirring it into ice cream soup.

Ice cream can be sculptured, too, by taking away or building up. Some creative eaters begin with a solid lump and carve shapes by spoon as they eat.

A few ice cream parlors are still noted for their ice cream constructions. They build tall towers of ice cream, shaping as they go with scoops, spades, spoons, and knives. They work fast!

Scoops and Dippers

Ice cream tastes great, and it looks appealing served in special imaginative ways. Over the years, inventors have thought up all kinds of dippers and scoops for making ice cream creations.

Once popular was a cone-shaped scoop with a little key on top. The key turned a scraper inside to pop the ice cream out.

Today, you can buy a plain ball scoop in the supermarket or variety store. If you dip it in water before you scoop, the ball of ice cream turns out easily. Another kind has a scraper inside, which you work by squeezing the handle or pressing on a thumb tab, and out drops a perfect ball of ice cream. These scoops come in different sizes. A scoop 2¾ inches in diameter is called No. 12 because it dips 12 balls from a quart of ice cream. Ice cream cones are usually dipped with a smaller scoop, No. 24, which

is 2 inches across. Another useful size, for dishes of ice cream or pie à la mode, is No. 16, 2½ inches across. Manufacturers make many more sizes for restaurants and ice cream parlors.

Ice cream dips best when it's 10 degrees above zero. It is soft enough to roll easily into a ball, but still doesn't melt too fast. Ice cream parlor clerks delight their buyers by adding a skirt to the ball— that's a fringe of extra ice cream.

Ice cream spades are shaped like paddles, and they have a sharp edge to cut through hard-frozen ice cream. Ice cream store clerks use spades to hand-pack ice cream in quart or pint cartons for you to take home.

When ice cream is really frozen hard, you may have to slice it with a knife, or wait while it softens.

FOUNTAINS...

The real magic of ice cream begins with creating exquisite concoctions. Not only can ice cream be flavored in hundreds of ways, but it also combines well with many foods and drinks.

Most of our old favorites—floats, sodas, sundaes, and malts—were invented in soda fountains and ice cream parlors over the past hundred years. Around the turn of the century, young and old gathered around the popular fountains to meet friends and eat the frozen feasts.

The soda jerk, magician of his day, served these special dishes with style. His magnificent "palace" had marble-top tables and counters, fancy wire ice cream chairs, and, sometimes, mirrored walls.

The first fountains were installed in drugstores, since carbonated water was originally sold by druggists as a remedy to cure this and that. The fountain contained the soda water and syrups which the clerks poured by jerking the handles.

AND FLOATS...

THE BLACK COW
Fill a glass half full with root beer. Drop in a scoop of vanilla ice cream. Fill with root beer and serve with a large straw. Part of the fun is poking the ice cream with the straw to help it melt.

THE RED POP TOP
Use red pop or cherry soda to fill a glass. Put in a large scoop of strawberry or vanilla ice cream. It turns pink.

COCA-LOLA
Pour cola into a glass and add a scoop of lemon or lime ice cream or sherbet. Fill the glass with cola. Yummm.

ORANGE GINGER FLOAT FOR 6
Mix 1½ cups cold orange juice and 2 (12-ounce) cans ginger ale. Pour into tall glasses. Add a scoop of chocolate ice cream to each glass. Sprinkle grated orange peel on top.

BELCH WATER and MOO JUICE

Jerk the fountain lever forward and out comes the carbonated soda water in a needle-hard spray. This fizzy jet stream helps to mix the milk, syrup, and ice cream in an ice cream soda. So the soda was called a *jerk*, and the fellow who made it, a *soda jerk*. "Jerk one!"

The soda jerks had fun inventing their own descriptive language. "Moo juice" tells you that milk comes from cows. "Belch water" is burpy soda water. A visit to a soda fountain today may not be so entertaining . . . but the concoctions are more popular than ever.

You can fizz sodas at home if you have a pressurized seltzer bottle. Or you can make do with a bottle of soda water. Open it and put your thumb over the opening. Shake the bottle. Then move your thumb just enough to let out a fizzy stream.

Hope your aim is good!

CHOCOLATE SODA

Put 2 or 3 tablespoons chocolate syrup into a tall glass. Add ¼ cup milk and a large scoop of chocolate or vanilla ice cream. Fill with soda water and stir.

FRUIT SODA

Put ⅓ cup crushed sweetened fruit into a tall glass. Use strawberries, raspberries, pineapple, or peaches. Add ¼ cup milk and a large scoop of ice cream—the same fruit ice cream or plain vanilla. Fill with soda water and stir.

LEMON SODA

Put 2 tablespoons frozen lemonade concentrate into a tall glass. Add a scoop of vanilla ice cream. Do not add milk—the acid in lemon juice curdles milk. Fill with soda water and stir.

HOW TO DRINK ICE CREAM

The secret of great shakes can now be revealed. Smooth thick shakes are not really shaken. They are machine-mixed. At the soda fountain, the mixer looks like a long rod with a small ruffled disk on the end. At home, the small blades of the blender do the best job. They blend the shake and make it fluffy. The big blades of an egg beater can't make a good shake.

Another secret is to have the milk ice cold. Syrups should be cold, too. But the ice cream should be slightly soft.

Blend on low speed and don't blend too long. Better a few lumps than to beat the air out.

Start with these formulas—then invent your own.

CHOCOLATE SHAKE

Put ¼ cup chocolate syrup into the blender with ¾ cup milk and 2 big scoops vanilla or chocolate ice cream. Blend 1 minute on low speed.

VANILLA SHAKE

Put ¾ cup milk and 2 big scoops of vanilla ice cream into the blender. Add 1 or 2 teaspoons of vanilla. Blend 1 minute on low speed.

STRAWBERRY SHAKE

Put ½ cup mashed, sweetened strawberries in the blender with ¾ cup milk and 2 scoops of strawberry or vanilla ice cream. Blend 1 minute on low speed.

BANANA VELVET FOR 6

Put into the blender 2 cups milk, 2 medium bananas, cut up, and 1 pint softened banana ice cream. Cover and blend at high speed 1 minute to chop bananas. Pour into chilled glasses and sprinkle with nutmeg.

MALTS, ANY FLAVOR

Malted milks are shakes with powdered malt added. Make it just like the other shakes and add 1 tablespoon of malted milk powder.

SUPER SHAKES

Do you dream of super-thick shakes so thick you need a large straw and a lot of suck to drink them? Plop straight ice cream of any flavor into the blender and give it a whirr.

Sundaes for Sundays

Sodas became so popular around the turn of the century that the Good People rose to combat this tempter. They got laws passed to forbid soda sales on Sundays. Not discouraged, soda fountain keepers started serving ice cream and syrup without the soda. They called their creation "sundae" and spelled it with an "e" so as not to offend.

To make sundaes, you need small bowls or glass sundae dishes. Put in a large scoop of vanilla or other flavor ice cream, pour on your favorite sauce, and decorate with a fluff of whipped topping. Add a cherry or a sprinkle of nuts.

HOT FUDGE SAUCE
½ cup cocoa (unsweetened)
1 cup sugar
1 cup light corn syrup
½ cup evaporated milk or light cream
3 tablespoons butter
¼ teaspoon salt
1 teaspoon vanilla

Mix the cocoa and sugar completely in a 2-quart saucepan. Stir in the corn syrup, evaporated milk or cream, butter, and salt. Place on stove; bring to a boil and boil on medium heat, stirring constantly, for 4 minutes. Remove from heat. Stir in the vanilla. Makes 2 cups.

BUTTERSCOTCH SAUCE

1¼ cups light brown sugar, firmly packed
1 cup light corn syrup
¼ cup butter
¼ teaspoon salt
½ cup evaporated milk
1 teaspoon vanilla

Mix together the brown sugar, corn syrup, butter, and salt in a 1-quart saucepan. Cook over medium heat, stirring constantly, until sugar dissolves. Do not boil. Cool to room temperature. Stir in the milk and vanilla and beat it with a spoon until well mixed. Makes 2 cups.

CARAMEL SAUCE

½ pound caramel candies (28 candies)
½ cup light or heavy cream

Unwrap the caramels and put them in the top of a double boiler with the cream. Stir over hot (not boiling) water until caramels melt and sauce is smooth.

Banana Split

Hey! Poke your finger into the end of a peeled banana and it splits into three! Lay the pieces on a plate and top with three scoops of ice cream. To duplicate the original old-time banana split, use one scoop each vanilla, chocolate, and strawberry. Spoon on pineapple sauce, chocolate sauce, and strawberry sauce. Decorate with whipped cream, nuts, and a cherry. Or do your own thing.

PINEAPPLE SAUCE
Drain an 8½-ounce can of crushed pineapple and mix it with 1 cup light corn syrup in a saucepan. Bring to a boil and cook until it thickens.

STRAWBERRY SAUCE
Mix ½ cup sugar and ½ cup water in a saucepan. Boil 5 minutes. Mash fresh or frozen strawberries. Stir in sugar syrup to taste.

RASPBERRY SAUCE
Thaw a 10-ounce package of frozen raspberries and push them through a sieve to remove seeds. Add sugar to taste. Mix 2 teaspoons cornstarch with a little of the juice to make a smooth paste. Stir paste into remaining juice. Cook and stir mixture over low heat until clear and slightly thickened.

Rules for the Super Party of the Year
1. Invite all your friends who like to eat.
2. Bring home several kinds of ice cream.
3. And sauces.
4. Don't forget toppings.
5. Or fruits and nuts, cherries, etc.
6. Be sure there's a dish and a spoon for everyone.

Everyone piles up any combination that looks appealing. It may run over the bowl in an icky mess, so give everyone a plate to put under the bowl.

RAINBOW SUNDAE

Ice cream·on·a·stick

One cold night in 1923, a man left a glass of lemonade on a window sill with a spoon in it. The next morning, there it was, frozen solid with the spoon for a handle. He had invented the Popsicle.

Want to make your own ice cream on a stick? Try this recipe:

1 cup orange, pineapple, or grape juice
½ cup sugar
⅛ teaspoon salt
¾ cup evaporated milk
1 tablespoon lemon juice

Mix the juice, sugar, and salt in a metal bowl or pan. Freeze to a mush. Chill the evaporated milk in the freezer for 1 hour. Whip it. Add the lemon juice and whip until stiff. Fold the fruit mush into whipped milk. Pour into 6 6-ounce metal juice cans, filling them ¾ full. Freeze to mushy, then push in a spoon, a plastic fork, or a wooden stick. Finish freezing. Run warm water on the can to pull out the ice cream.

Fleets of ice cream trucks ringing bells visit city neighborhoods in the warm months. "Hey, Dad. Catch the ice cream man!"

Manufacturers solved the problem of how to make melted chocolate stick to ice cream. The secret—if you want to do it at home—is to keep the chocolate from getting too hot.

Cut the ice cream into bars about $1\frac{1}{2}$ inches thick and $2\frac{1}{2}$ inches long. Push a stick into each bar and put in the freezer to harden.

In a double sandwich bag (one inside the other), put 1 tablespoon vegetable shortening and a 4-ounce milk chocolate bar, broken up. Seal the bag tightly with a twist-tie. Put it in a bowl of hot tap water to melt—it takes about 15 minutes. Knead the bag gently to mix melted chocolate and shortening and pour it into a small bowl. With a table knife, spread chocolate over ice cream—like buttering bread. Watch the chocolate harden! Eat it now or store in the freezer. One chocolate bar coats 3 ice cream bars.

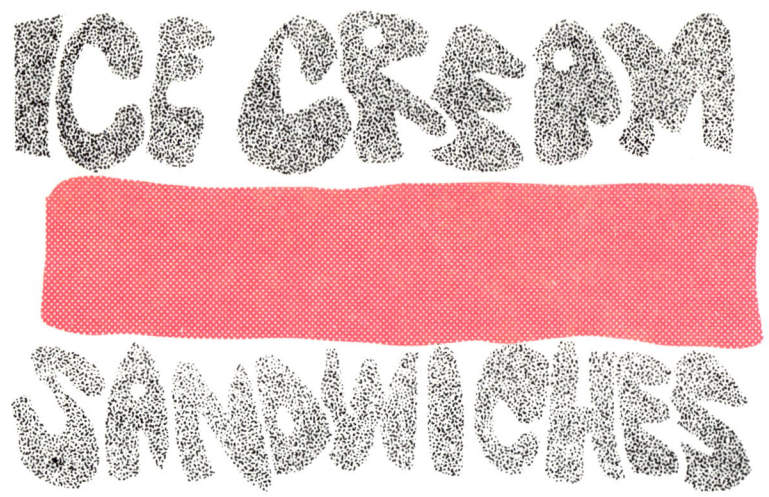

ICE CREAM SANDWICHES

When you're out of cones, you can improvise by making ice cream sandwiches. There are lots of ideas for the sandwich part—and you avoid dishwashing, too.

Use a wet knife to cut thin slices of ice cream—half an inch is about right unless you have a good-sized mouth.

If you are making several sandwiches for your friends, slice the ice cream and put the slices back in the freezer to harden. Put the sandwiches together when you are ready to eat them.

1. Sandwich the ice cream between cookies.
2. Or between cinnamon graham crackers.
3. Crisp waffles or waffle cookies make super sandwiches.
4. Popcorn balls, molded into patties, taste great with ice cream.

snow balls

For snowballs in the summer, scoop ice cream into balls and coat them with coconut or something else that's crunchy or crispy. Serve them in dessert dishes with your favorite sauce.

Here's what to do so you don't make a gooey mess of it. As fast as you make the balls, put them in a shallow pan and into the freezer to harden. Put the coating in another shallow pan. When the balls are hard again, roll them in the coating. Keep them frozen until dessert time.

For colored coconut snowballs, mix ½ teaspoon milk and a few drops of food coloring in a bowl. Add a can of flaked coconut and toss until the color looks even.

Other coatings to try: chopped nuts, cookie or graham cracker crumbs, crushed peppermint candy, or crushed peanut brittle.

HAPPY BIRTHDAY

Ice cream and cake say "Birthday Party." But there are plenty of unbirthday times when you can serve it.

Try these combinations of cake and ice cream together, or invent your own. A gourmet cook (pronounced *goor-may*) is an artist in the kitchen, putting together exciting tastes and attractive arrangements of food.

DOUBLE DEVIL'S FOOD
Bake 2 round layers of chocolate cake mix or your own recipe. Spread the cooled bottom layer with chocolate ice cream, as thick as you wish. Pop the other layer on top. Freeze about 1 hour to firm it. Pour chocolate sauce over the slices when you serve it.

SPICY NUT
Bake 2 square pans of spice cake from a mix or from scratch. (That means measuring all the ingredients yourself.) Spread the cooled cake with butter pecan ice cream. Harden in the freezer. Top the servings with whipped cream.

FOOL-THE-EYE CAKE
Skip the cake part and frost the ice cream. A pint, quart, or half-gallon brick, frozen very hard, makes a great fake cake.

For a different shape cake, pack softened ice cream into a cake pan or mold. Freeze until hard. To get it out, dip the mold in warm water and turn ice cream out onto a cold plate.

TO YOU AND ME AND EVERYBODY

To frost a half-gallon size "cake," whip 2 cups chilled heavy cream until stiff. Tint a quarter of it with a drop or two of food color and put it into a decorating tube. Now work fast! Unwrap ice cream and spread with whipped cream. Trim with tinted cream and hurry it back to the freezer.

I CALL 'EM GOOD

The French call them *crêpes*, the English say griddle cakes, and American woodsmen ask for flapjacks. In Mexico they are tortillas, and in Russia they are blini. Whatever you call pancakes, they taste delicious with ice cream.

This recipe makes thin pancakes which are easy to roll around a scoop of ice cream.

   1 cup biscuit mix
   1 egg
   1 cup milk

Beat all ingredients together in a bowl until smooth. Heat griddle to 380° (or until a drop of water dances on it). Pour ¼ cup batter on the griddle. As soon as bubbles show and cake is brown when you peek underneath, turn it over and brown the other side. Put it on a plate and roll it around a scoop of vanilla ice cream. Pour on warm orange marmalade thinned with maple syrup.

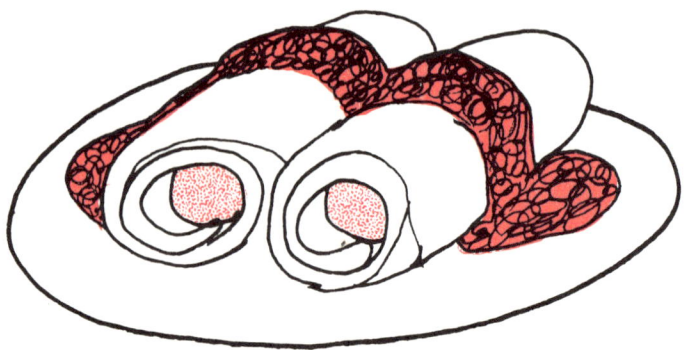

One way to make ice cream pie is to butter a piepan and sprinkle it with ½ cup cookie crumbs. Cut slices of slightly softened ice cream and fit them into the pan. Then smooth with the back of a spoon. Freeze until firm. Cut in wedges and serve with your favorite sauce.

For crumbs you can use chocolate wafers, gingersnaps, vanilla wafers, or cinnamon graham crackers.

Or turn this idea upside down and use the ice cream for the pie crust. Spread a thick layer of vanilla ice cream in a piepan. Freeze until firm. Fill with orange sherbet. Or try peach ice cream crust with raspberry sherbet.

Make Molds

Molded ice cream shapes look like toys that you can eat. Molds for different holidays help celebrate the day. Strawberry pink ice cream in a heart-shaped mold makes a valentine. Green mint ice cream in shamrock shapes says St. Patrick's Day. Wreaths and Santa shapes mean Christmas. People or animal molds say that any day is a good day for a special way to eat ice cream. Many of the early ice cream molds came from Germany. You can use gelatin molds, cookie cutters, plastic or metal molds. You can even make shapes from heavy foil.

The fanciest way to mold ice cream is to put one design inside another. For example, fill a little star-shaped cutter with chocolate ice cream. Freeze until hard. Hold your warm fingers around the mold until you can push the ice cream out. Refreeze. Put a big round cutter on a foil pan and put the chocolate star in the middle. Spoon softened vanilla ice cream around it and put it back in the freezer to harden. Remove the round mold and you have a patty of ice cream with a star in the middle.

To decorate molded shapes, use squeeze-on frosting in tubes.

IT'S A BOMBE!

Big molds make beautiful spectaculars. The bombe is a French invention; it uses two or more flavors and colors of ice cream. When you slice through it, everyone sees the layers inside.

PISTACHIO CRUNCH BOMBE
- ¾ cup corn flake crumbs
- ½ cup flaked coconut
- ¼ cup chopped toasted peanuts
- ¼ cup sugar
- ¼ cup butter, softened
- 1 quart vanilla ice cream, slightly softened
- 1 pint pistachio ice cream, slightly softened

With your hands, mix together the crumbs, coconut, peanuts, sugar, and butter. Press onto the bottom and sides of a fancy 7-cup mold. Spread vanilla ice cream over the crumb shell. Harden in the freezer. Fill the center with pistachio ice cream and freeze again. Dip into warm water to unmold and turn out on a chilled plate. Harden again in the freezer. Pour on chocolate sauce. Makes 10 to 12 servings. Great!

WOULD YOU EAT A MOOSE?

You can eat this mousse spelled the French way with a "u." It's a foamy, light, whipped dessert.

  2 cups heavy cream, chilled
  ½ cup sifted confectioners' sugar
  ¼ teaspoon salt
  1 cup chocolate syrup

Pour the chilled cream into a chilled 2-quart bowl. Add the sugar and salt. Whip until stiff. Pour the chocolate syrup over the whipped cream and fold them together. Folding is a lighter, gentler way of mixing than beating or stirring. Pour the mixture into foil baking cups set in muffin pans. Freeze until firm. Makes 15 cups of mousse.

PARFAITS

Many French people fled their country after the French Revolution and came to the United States. They brought elegant ice cream recipes. One of their creations that we love for parties and banquets is the parfait (*par-fay*).

The American parfait is a dressed-up sundae in a tall skinny stemmed glass. Fill the glass ahead of time with layers of ice cream and fruit or sauce that taste good and look pretty together. Store in the freezer until dessert time. Decorate with whipped cream and a cherry or other garnish.

Hot and Cold

One of the most heavenly ways to enjoy ice cream is in a strawberry shortcake. Make the shortcake from biscuit mix or from ingredients in the cupboard. While it's baking, heat frozen strawberries in a pan on the stove. Split each biscuit and put each bottom half in a small bowl. Pour on some strawberry juice. Add a scoop of vanilla ice cream and cover with biscuit top. Pour hot strawberries over all and crown the whole beautiful thing with whipped topping and a whole strawberry jewel.

That's so good, why not try other shortcakes? See what's in the pantry. You can heat peaches until the juice thickens to syrup and pour over spongecake and chocolate ice cream. Or heat fruit pie fillings—cherry or blueberry. Wouldn't cinnamon ice cream be good with apple pie filling and grated cheese?

Ice cream all day long

Ice cream makes a tasty tongue-teaser nearly anytime with nearly anything.

1. Assemble a cereal sundae for breakfast.
2. For lunch, load a hollow melon middle with ice cream. Or fill a scooped-out orange shell and pile on more sliced fruit.
3. Make a different dinner dessert. Put ice cream on pear halves and pour on hot chocolate sauce. Gourmets call this Pears Helene. Peach Melba, invented to honor a famous opera star, is a peach half, a scoop of vanilla, and raspberry sauce.
4. What under the sun, moon, and stars can you eat with ice cream? How about ice cream with raisins? With nuts or candy bits? An orange juice float? Doughnut split? Honey peanut-butter shake? Praline parfait?

Carolyn Vosburg Hall remembers "Sunday afternoons when we were children—the big treat was to pile in the car and drive to Clarkston for ice cream cones. My brother always gobbled his, but my sister and I licked as slowly as we could to make it last all the way home."

A busy artist, writer, and mother of three, Mrs. Hall now has a difficult time making ice cream last—someone in the family is always digging into the half-gallons she stores in the freezer. "My husband, Cap, loves ice cream. We've eaten *gelati* in Italy, asked for *aisu kurimu* in Japan, and admired fabulous bombes in Paris."

This book is the second in a series for children written in collaboration with FARM JOURNAL editors. The first was *I Love Popcorn*.

Farm families—the food producers of America—want young people to know where their food comes from and what it does for health. The FARM JOURNAL staff supplied facts about milk and ice cream production and nutrition and perfected recipes in the magazine's test kitchens.

Carolyn Hall holds degrees in painting and design from Cranbrook Academy of Art in Birmingham, Michigan; she has taught children's classes at the Detroit Institute of Art. She is the author of *Stitched and Stuffed Art*. Her own soft sculpture stitchery and paintings have been exhibited in many galleries and one-woman shows.